Dear Mom and Dad,
      Please, you have to get me out of here. You are the only ones that can do it. It's not that I'm just homesick, it's a word farther then that. I have to get out of here. I promise you, if you don't get me out of here, I'll run away. Please! I'm not kidding. Mom! Dad! I love you. Get me out of here.

                              Love,
                              Jim

P.S.: Please talk to my counslers, I just don't belong here.

P.S. still I^ HATE IT HERE!

P.S. still I^HATE IT HERE!

MORE KIDS' LETTERS FROM CAMP

Selected and edited by Diane Falanga

Abrams Image
New York

Contents

Foreword

By Diane Falanga

If you read the original collection, *P.S. I Hate It Here: Kids' Letters from Camp*, you'll know why I jumped at the chance to select and edit more kids' camp letters. And if you didn't read the first volume, there's still time!

I may have one of the all-time greatest jobs: spending my time reading thousands of hilarious camp letters and sharing the best bits with anyone who will listen. Through it all, I've developed a full-blown camp-letter addiction. I can't seem to get enough of these kids and their ability to say it like it is.

Some of the laugh-out-loud notes in this book were written over fifty years ago. In the current era of computerized and digitalized everything, our kids' rare, handwritten gems are cherished all the more. But no matter the year, a common thread unites them: The words are pure, the thoughts are unfiltered, and the emotions are raw and honest. These writers are sophisticated innocents, able to evoke pathos with sheer humor.

The idea of compiling a book of camp letters first took root when my now teenage daughter, Bianca, was a bright-eyed, brand-new, eight-year-old camper (euphemism for "homesick camp kid"). Her tearful, hyperbolic first letter home, "We have chores today. I am the Scraper, Sweeper and Maid," left me wracked with guilt and weepy, but also belly-laughing.

It inspired me to kick off a nationwide email chain to friends, family, and camps to look for more sidesplitting letters, hoping to spread the humor—and to help homesick kids see that they're not alone.

In *P.S. I Still Hate It Here*, meet Sarina on page 11 who writes, "I love everything about this camp except the campers." And Eli on page 42 who reports, "I am having a great time at camp, but I am a wreck." There's Gary on page 21 who sends the simple update "The food is great and I change my underwear." And Bruno (page 148), working on his English at summer language camp in Milan, who describes his homesickness to his parents: "I am like one shower without water and you are plumber."

For those of you who enjoyed *P.S. I Hate It Here*, here are some quick camper updates:

p. 10: The rash on Josh's P-Nus improved. All's great with his running, and he started saying the word "eggs" again.

p. 11: Stanton is still alive.

p. 25: Rachel outgrew her retainer.

p. 39: More weirdly bad stuff happened to Nicki. But she still didn't cry.

p. 73: Leslie's hair grew back. Just not quite as thick.

p. 86: Nick got out on bail.

As with the first volume, this second book is a collection of actual camp letters written home by kids—most getting a taste of independence for the very first time. Please enjoy this hysterical portal into the hearts and minds of kids spending the summer away at camp. For all of you who've been in their shoes, I hope this trip down memory lane brings laughter and heartfelt memories.

News from Camp

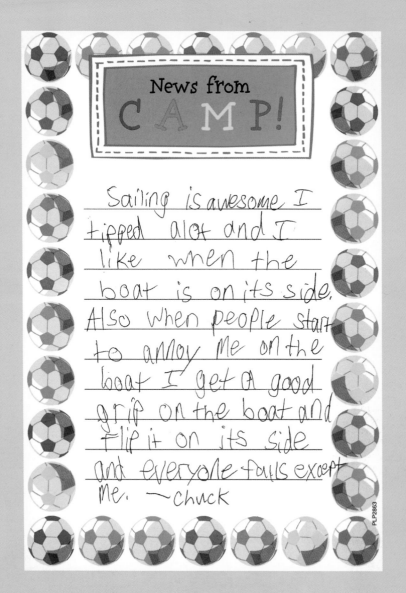

News from CAMP!

Sailing is awesome I tipped alot and I like when the boat is on its side. Also when people start to annoy me on the boat I get a good grip on the boat and flip it on its side and everyone falls except me. ~ Chuck

PLP2863

Dear Mimi,

I miss you so much. I love your london card you sent. It's so cute. I can't believe in two days we leave and get to see you. It's sad and happy at the same time. I've got to go plunge a toilet. Bye.

love Mckay

Dear Mom and Dad,
I love everything
about this camp... except
the ~~connectors~~ campers.
Love,
Sarina

WHEN YOU'RE GONE THE WORLD'S A EMPTY OLE PLACE!

DEAR MOM
I'M THE LEAST LIKED IN
THE HOLE CABIN OUR
COUNCELOR IS MEAN AND
HE YELLS AT ME MOST. I
MISS YOU AND I WANT
TO GO HOME

BY NOW DAVID

X X X X X X
O O O O O O

Dear Mom,
I hate Riflery a Bird flew by
my target and
and I think I didn't know
if fell!!! I shot it becaus
my gun'. the women took
and shoot my targ
for the rest of the class.
Love Lindy!!

<u>HI</u> MOM + KARYN + DONNA +PIPS, WED 4 (EVERYBODY)

EVERYTHING'S OKEY HERE YESTERDAY
I TRIED TO PASS A SWIMMING
TEST THE HIGHEST ONE I ~~ALMOST~~
FLUNKED. TODAY I TRIED FOR ~~XX~~
THE ~~HIGHEST~~ SECOND HIGHEST
ONE AND I DID IT. WE ALSO WENT
ON A HIKE YESTERDAY AND CAUGHT
A RABBIT BUT IT DIED OF RABBIES
MIKE NATURE (THE NATURE COUNCLER)
GOT SCRACHTED BY IT AND GOT
SOME NEEDLES I'V GOT MILLIONES
OF MISCETO BITS ON MY
BACK AND I LOST THE
KEY TO MY TRUNK SO.
PLEASE TRY TO SEND ME
ANOTHER I NEED IT. IT
LOOK SOMETHING (MORE→)

...MY HEART GETS THAT EMPTY FEELING, WHEN YOU'RE AWAY!

14

LIKE THIS 🔑 ~~███~~ I ONLY THINK
I'M NOT ~~██~~ POSOTIVE

    SIGNING OFF YOUR SON
    + BROTER ~~████████~~
       ↓
        David

P.S. WRITE LOTS + LOTS
OF LETTERS AND STUFF
P.P.S I MISS YOU ALOUT
<u>BUT</u> I'M HAVING FUN.

Dear Everyone,

In Pocohontis I guess
What I am? I'm a
Interpeting dancing LEAF!
I must really stink @ acting!

Love
Lydia

16

6/19/06

Dear Mom and Dad,
I'm having a great
time at camp. The food
is ~~xxxx~~ good. My conslers
are relly nice. Last
night I only got 4 hours
of sleep, because of these
~~xxxx~~ two kids, Nick and AJ.
They would not stop talking.

Love,
Will

Dear Mom and Dad,

I am writing you this letter during the morning of June 26. My previous letter (postcard) stated that I rated Camp. So far a 4. I will tell you what I rate each individual thing:

Bus Ride - 8

Off Bus → Haircheck - 4

First impresions of bunk - 3

Heat - 0

Unpack - 3

Dinner - 8
→ Afterdinner activity - 0
Bed - 5

Love,
Noah

Dear Mom and Dad,

Last night, a staff member went over some rules. Here are some importaint rules:

No iPod with video aloud.

All candy (except gum) must be eaten by Saturday.

No electronics except for: watches, iPads with no video.

These are some rules to keep in mind for next year.

Love,
Noah

P.S. No candy thas is not kosher is aloud. Also, no peanuts are aloud.

Camp

news

Dear Mom + Dad,

I got all of your lovely letter. They are good and funny stories, thanks! I get all of them at Lunch the day after you send them. I have made a lot of friends. Except for one. Everyone dousn't like him, (or should I said didn't like him.) His name was Brandan and was mean to everyone, Not just me, don't worry. He tried to run away 3 times _____. Finally after all of his stupid complaining he left camp on Monday, (the day before waterpark day)!! Everyone was happy, even his parents, They said "Now you guys can finally have fun." Think god he's gone.

Love Danny

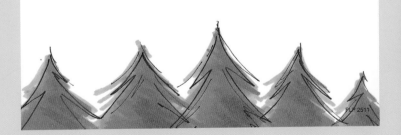

Dear Mom, Dad + Marty,
I am having a swell time.
~~Somone~~ Someone copped my flash light
The food is great, and I change
my underware.

Love,
GARY

Dear Marty,
Thank you for the confidense you
gave me about beating the lousy
~~head~~ head in of the guy who
swiped ~~it~~ my flashlight but its
a big cam and ~~I~~ ~~don~~ doughts
I'll find the thief.

Love GARY

hi! I have been
sending letters every day
but they take a while to get
to you guys. It getting
better but little to cristian
for me. I think two weeks
would be enough. I'm
kinda bored. My feet smell.
Today it was warm with
sun. Tomorrow we get
a lazy day so we get to
sleep late. AND GET DONUTS.
so dad you can have a donut.
I'm starting to miss you
guys less. Sing a happy song.
I dont like broccoli. They keep
serving it and its killing me
slowly.

bye
♡ Carly

Dear Mommy & Daddy,   Tuesday

I wrote you a letter before that I wanted to come home but now I feel so much better. Today we went tubing it was so much fun, and we have to clean the bathrooms, but guess what?... We don't have to clean the toilets.

Love,
Hilary

By the way Dad, I know that this is a CO-ED camp, but all the boys are ugly, dorky and blech ¼. So no need to worry.

I ♡ all of you, and I miss you so much already!

♡ Arielle

24

I Just Had lunch and we had
Hanbergers! I Have the best cabin
we fake farted all night.

Max

Dear mom, dad, &blake,
I am **writing** to you like an amish girl cause
im using a feather pen + ink.

Bianca

Dear Mom+Dad

I just had the best sloppy joe in the world. I ate so much I almost puked. I went fishing for the first time yesterday and again today. Yesterday Max cout to fish in like five minites. I had to get my casters aproved before I could fish. Max has been alot nicer to me in the past few day. I did maca 2nd period. We made ROOT BEER. It was so good. All of max's friend looked so different than I imagaened but nice. I have pooped so don't worry. I am still trying to get the way of camp. I know that this is weird but can you pleas send me those sticky cushy thing so the door to the cabin dose not slam.

Love,
Charlie

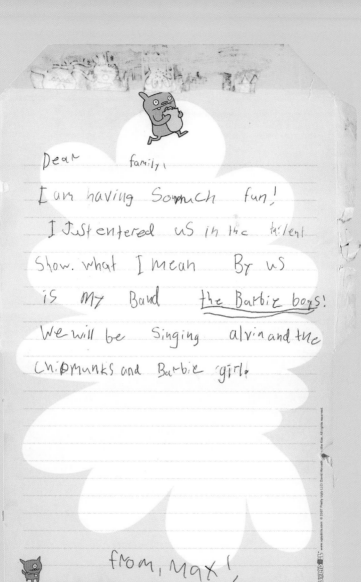

Dear family,

I am having so much fun!

I just entered us in the talent show. what I mean By us is my Band the Barbie boys!

We will be singing alvin and the chipmunks and Barbie girl.

from, Max!

Page 1

Danielle

1st Day

Mom + Dad,

I am sorry to worry you but I hate it here. ~~XXX~~ I am the ~~XX~~ oldest in my cabin. Every one is at least under 4 feet tall! I am on the bottom bunk. My conslers are really nice though. Line (pronounced ~~X~~ Linn) is really nice. She (sorry to say this Mom) has her tonge peirced. The other one (I don't know her name) is O.K.

When I got to camp and found my cabin group I freeked out! I ~~XXX XXXX~~ ~~the~~ have never ever seen smaller people in my life!

Love Always,
Danielle

hi! do you guys
like my postcard.
Todays we got
POP...soda and
candy it was
tasty... I killed
a lot of mosquites
and learned how
to use a gun
bye have fun!
Carly

Hi Mom!. Dad

I lost my notebook
collidiously. I'm going bowling
today.

Andy

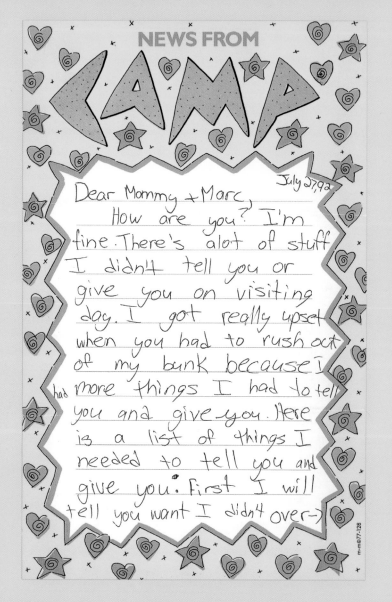

NEWS FROM CAMP

July 27,92

Dear Mommy + Marc,
    How are you? I'm fine. There's a lot of stuff I didn't tell you or give you on visiting day. I got really upset when you had to rush out of my bunk because I had more things I had to tell you and give you. Here is a list of things I needed to tell you and give you. First I will tell you want I didn't over→

give you. List: fan, film, some books, my tennis balls, blow drier and my rain boots and Keds. List for things to tell you: I need a white head band, I have a hole in my sleeping bag, I didn't show you my whole camp, I can't eat certain foods because they hurt my stomach, tell Linda to tell Liza to write back because I wrote to her and she never wrote back, tell Randy to write back, Mel said Lauren can't come with me and Daddy, I love the stationary you got me, I love my troll, I heard Star Light hasn't gone to any gym meets this summer and they have been cheating and I miss you alot and can't wait to see you again and cry when I think about you. I can't wait to go shopping with you again. I miss you soooooo much. I love you sooo much.   P.S
P.S. Marc say Hi to   Nina & Ben   Love,   say Hi to everyone at work espkcally   Eryn   Cary & Todd

31

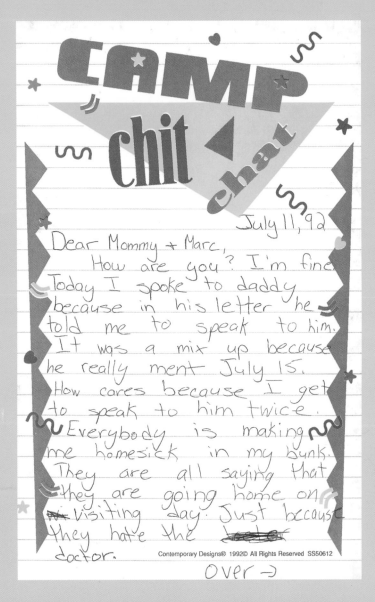

CAMP chit chat

July 11, 92

Dear Mommy + Marc,
How are you? I'm fine.
Today I spoke to daddy
because in his letter he
told me to speak to him.
It was a mix up because
he really ment July 15.
How cares because I get
to speak to him twice.
Everybody is making
me homesick in my bunk.
They are all saying that
they are going home on
visiting day. Just because
they hate the ~~doctor~~
doctor.

Over →

I hate the doctor to but I don't think that's a reason to go home. The reason I hate him is because he is old and doesn't care about anyone. He is not a good doctor. I really miss and cry every night because my bunk is making me homesick. I can't wait to see you and speak to you. I love you and miss you alot.

Love,
Eryn

P.S.
write back

Dear Mom + Dad,
I am horrible! I'm soaked in sweat. I also really need to pee # poop

Come visit soon!
XXXXXooooo
Owen

Dear Mom + Dad,   7-17-11
Never mind 'bout the bathroom
there's a huge thunderstorm and
I'm so freaked out. It looks
like 8:30 PM but it's only 2:35 PM
and I saw some flashes of lightning
and I miss you guys so so so much!
XXXXXXXXXXX XXX X X XX XXXX
OOOOOOOOOOOOO OOOOOO OOOO

Dear Mom + Dad,
My new worry is my bites, the
heat, and the bugs. The heat
is unbearable! I miss you so so so much
If dad has updates please send
me them.
XXXXXXXXX X X X OOOOOO OO OO
Owen

From: To:
Date: Camp:

Someone who loves you sent you this REPLY FORM. It works just like a fax. All you need to do is write a letter in the box below and hand it in with the rest of your mail. (Don't fold it or wrinkle it.) We will fax this form directly back to Bunk1 and on to whoever sent it to you. It's just like getting email and writing back, so write back as soon as you can! The faster you answer, the faster we can send it back
Write your message below in blue or black ink - NO PENCIL

Hi Mom, Hi Dad,

Next time I should bring more shorts and my armpits are a little bumpy what do I do? Today is lazy day which means i dont have any classes and we have super cabin clean up which means is when you do a super doper cabin clean up while music is playing and we get to glaze our pottery today! !!!!!

Lindsay

Love u

36

BUNK REPLY STATIONERY

From: To:

Date: Camp:

Someone who loves you sent you this REPLY FORM. It works just like a fax. All you need to do is write a letter in the box below and hand it in with the rest of your mail. (Don't fold it or wrinkle it.) We will fax this form directly back to Bunk1 and on to whoever sent it to you. It's just like getting email and writing back, so write back as soon as you can! The faster you answer, the faster we can send it back

Write your message below in blue or black ink - NO PENCIL

Hi moms Hi dad,

waterskiing actually doesn't have anything to do with snow skiing! And I got a package from someone but i dont know who its from. I got some bug bites but there not itchy (yay)

I'm not going to the new Harry potter because I want to finish the Books first All my cabin mates are my friend except one ill tell U about her l8R I have 2 new BFFs named Sophie and Olivia There not going to the movie either! my armpits dont itch!

Love U

Lindsay

Camp

ELKHORN, WISCONSIN 53121

July 30, 1969

Dear Pat,

Have you been working hard?
I've been doing lots of things. I'm
too tired to tell about all of them.
I'll just tell you about our cool
sock hop. It was real dumb. I
didn't like it a bit. I was the
only one who didn't dance. It
was DUMB!

Well
Byyyyyy!

Love,
Judy

CAMP   HAMMONDSPORT, N. Y
                        July 31, 1966

I challenged Debbie to this one
game that was called "Ready Marity"
or something like that.   with one
hand, we'd each hold one end of a stick.
then, we'd be blind-folded and
one guy would duck his head, then
the other guy would try and
hit his head with a rolled
up newspaper which was in his
other hand. I hit Debbie once
in the head, once in the knees, and
once in the shoulders. She hit me
twice in the knees and once on
the shoulders. I did a back bend
two times and those were the
times she hit me in the knees.
I won for my team.
                    Bye,
                    Love, Cindy

39

♡ Samantha ♡

Dear mom & Dad
I m got to camp
safley I'm in Buck
fern I got here
& I am not

Dead

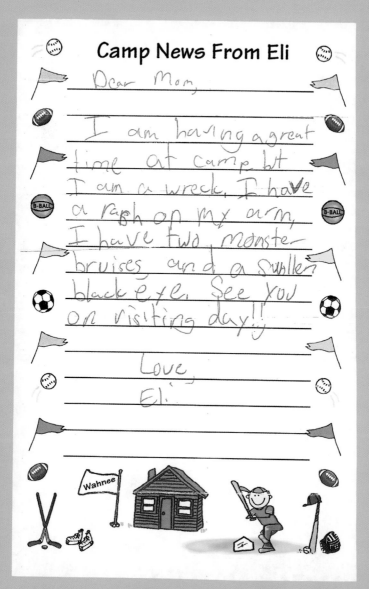

Camp News From Eli

Dear Mom,

I am having a great time at camp, but I am a wreck. I have a rash on my arm, I have two monster bruises and a swollen black eye. See you on visiting day!!

Love,
Eli

Camp News From Eli

Dear Mom,

I am enjoying camp, but I have a question. Can you search "How to prevent eye crust"? I get too much and every couple days, I can't open my eyes without peeling it all of first. Thank you.

Love
Eli

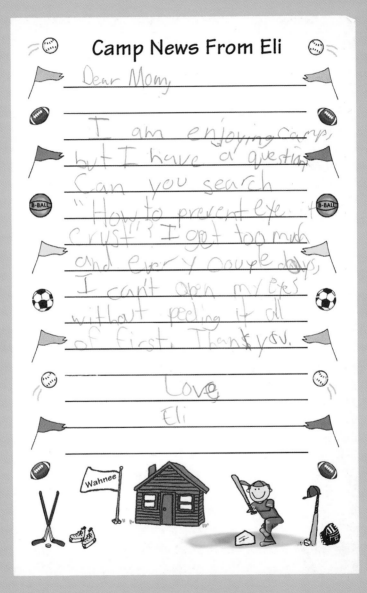

Dear every one,

last night I found out that I had

a tick. It was on my foot so I

liped to the eamfermey Iliped so

my vaens would not send

extra Bb00lto my leg so the

tick could drink it. It was

a wood tick. the nerse took it out

veats quick and then I berned it!

from,

Dear Mom + Dad,

It is exstreamly hot and humid. My legs look much worse than last year and are very bloody.

Love,
Charlie

Dear Mom and day
tonight was and not I my
lucky night, First I spilled
the hole entire plate of
meatloof on me and the
got all this bb-Q sauce on
me, the the jello fell
on me and I got all
sticky, and last I got a cup
of water on me and
I has wet, But camp
is still fun, I forgot
to say this but John from
(my counser) is
chicago, He is very his
and so is my other
counsler, I

Love you,
Jake

Mom,
Thursday "Aunt Rose" visited. I may run out of supplies. Aunt Rose has visited a lot of ppl in our cabin since we live together. ~~I won't the to~~ I can't go swimming. I'd get stained. I'm speaking in code!

Bye! -Kristine

P.S. I love you

Hey Mom,
I'm writing this on July 15th, in case you sent me other mail. Could you also (if you get this) tell me what our zip code is? The first few days of camp were fun, but I'm sick now and I feel terrible. I think I'm probably going to throw up sometime today, it keeps almost happening. Also, I think I lost the other postcard, but I'll buy new ones from the camp store.

So if this is the only letter you get from me please don't stop writing. I miss you guys, but at least my book is great! Love, Theo

Dear Mom+Dad,

I just wokeup, because there were flies buzzing in my ear. our cabin is so dirty and un-clean, that this bacterial desicase called Empitiga. so far 4 people in our cabin have it under there arpits. I have it all over my face and starting to get a bunch under my armpits. It's super contagious. I am getting a big puffy wort on my knee and it hurts. The nurses treated is terribly.

©stephen joseph

Th Empitiga

48

Hi People!

- Jess got stepped on by a horse but is okay now.
- Then, at basketball and a girl threw a ball at her mouth and it hit her lip/ braces. She was bleeding pretty bad but is okay now.
- I was playing basketball too and my thumb got jammed and swolen but I'm okay now.
- Lilach's saddle ~~fell~~ slipped and she fell off her horse.

♡, Juliet

Dear, mom, and dad.
I'm not going to write
much because I'm really
tierd! well today
was fun, I'm kind
of clumsy. so, you know
how I tend to get
things in my eye? well,
today during dinner
I got Tobasco sauce in
my eye! I'm better now,
so you don't have to
worry?

love, Zack!

BUNK REPLY STATIONERY

From: To:
Date: Camp:

Someone who loves you sent you this REPLY FORM. It works just like a fax. All you need to do is write a letter in the box below and hand it in
with the rest of your mail. (Don't fold it or wrinkle it.) We will fax this form directly back to Bunk1 and on to whoever sent it to you. It's just like
getting email and writing back, so write back as soon as you can! The faster you answer, the faster we can send it back
Write your message below in blue or black ink - NO PENCILS

Dear Mom and Dad,
Yesterday I sprained my ankle and the nurses gave
me crutches. Also I have a loose tooth.

                                         Jackie

BUNK REPLY STATIONERY

From: To:
Date: Camp:

Someone who loves you sent you this REPLY FORM. It works just like a fax. All you need to do is write a letter in the box below and hand it in
with the rest of your mail. (Don't fold it or wrinkle it.) We will fax this form directly back to Bunk1 and on to whoever sent it to you. It's just like
getting email and writing back, so write back as soon as you can! The faster you answer, the faster we can send it back
Write your message below in blue or black ink - NO PENCIL

Dear Mom,
I forgot to say something in the last letter.
I had an ear infection, so the health center went to
the pharmacy and got me a pill bottle of antibiotics
for it. No other news.

                                         From,
                                         Jackie

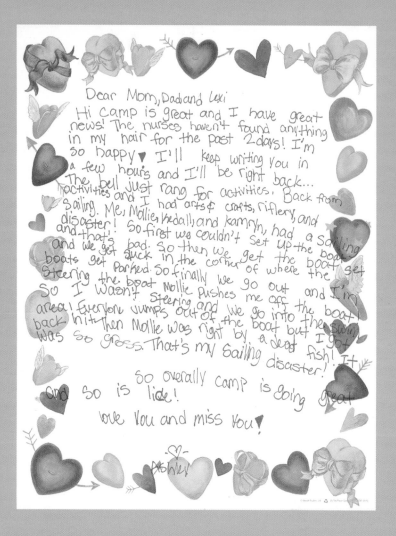

Dear Mom, Dad and Lexi

Hi camp is great and I have great news! The nurses haven't found anything in my hair for the past 2 days! I'm so happy ♥ I'll keep writing you in a few hours and I'll be right back...

The bell just rang for activities. Back from activities and I had arts & crafts, riflery, and sailing. Me, Mollie, Kedall, and Kamryn, had a sailing disaster! So first we couldn't set up the boat and that's bad. So then we get the boat set and we get stuck in the corner of where the boats get parked. So finally we go out and I'm steering the boat Mollie pushes me off the boat! So I wasn't steering and we go into the swim area! Everyone jumps out of the boat but I got back in. Then Mollie was right by a dead fish! It was so gross. That's my sailing disaster!

So overall camp is going great and so is life!

love you and miss you!

Ashley

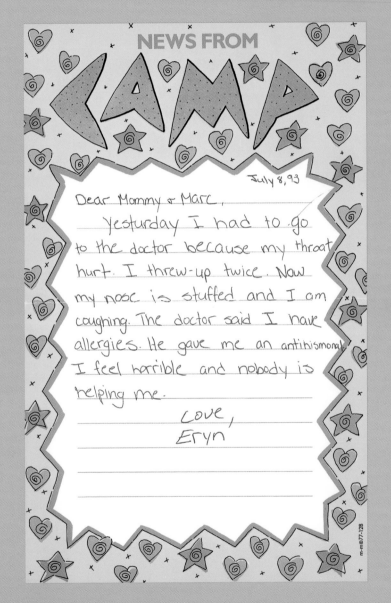

NEWS FROM CAMP

July 8, 93

Dear Mommy & Marc,

Yesturday I had to go to the doctor because my throat hurt. I threw-up twice. Now my nose is stuffed and I am coughing. The doctor said I have allergies. He gave me an antihismoml. I feel horrible and nobody is helping me.

Love,
Eryn

Dear Mom
I think I have a feaver,
and a infectid foot. But any-
way, Great Lakes got in third
place. I ~~signd~~ signed
up for the snepper over
nighter. I won three events
in pell ~~ounoun~~ Day

From,
Charlie
M

Peace ♥ Camp

8/1/10

Dear Mom + Dad,
Everyone has been
getting hurt / visiting
the nurses office!
One girl threw-up,
another girl's eyes
started swelling, one
got hit in the face with
a frisbee, someone else
smashed their finger in
a bowling ball, another
girl's hand swelled
up, + another couldn't
sleep because of the
springy mattress.
But aren't ya proud
of me? I WASN'T
A PART IN ANY
OF THIS! I ♥
U! LOVe,
Isabelle

Dear Mommy
Can you try to
make one more
phone call. Theres
something I want
to talk about.
I saw Dr. Dick.
He gave me
something to take
for my allergies.
I took it for
two daies. I found
my flash light.
But I didnt find
my sticker books
yet. Barrie didnt
even ask the bunk
to look. Cam you
speak to her. I love you

Dear Mom and Dad,
I just came back from a wild trip because their was a tornado on our lake that we stalled on. Their was 75 mph wind blowing. It was the scariest time of my life. Will had a huge Oak tree fall on his tent. But everthing is fine. Can't wait for you to come here.
                                        Love,
                                        John

Dear Marc,   July 9,93
    This is a quick letter because I need one to get into dinner. Last night I saw "Sleepless In seatle". It was pretty good. I'll tell you more about tomarrow. Today my wire on the top of my jaw got bent. It hurts when I chew. It is digging into my jaw. Tomarrow a girl in my bunk, her parents are coming up to visit Mel & Herb. Her parents are dentist so they are going to fix it for me. I think I must have ate something to hard. I will watch myself. I won't eat hard things anymore. By the way yesturday I went once around the whole lake on the rope. I love you and miss you. Love, Eryn

July 11, 93

Dear Mommy,

Hi. How are you? Today I spoke to Daddy because of the wire across the roof of my mouth. Somehow it got pushed up into my pallet and now it is stuck. I can't chew because it really hurts when I do. I have been eating breakfast but not Lunch or Dinner. I have only eaten bread for Lunch and Dinner. I have to suck on my food. I have a little cold because I am coughing and sniffiling a little. I went to the doctor and he told me I have alergies probably. He said the snot is running down my throat and making me cough. It has gotten much better. I take Tryaminic. The new doctor works at a hospitial during the day.

BORN TO
COWDILLAC
MOO!

August 17, 92

Dear Marc,
    How are you? I'm fine.
I have a cold. I cough alot
and my noise is stuffed.
I'm taking medicine. My tooth
fell out yesturday and know
I have a space in my mouth.

Love,   I Love you
Eryn.   ♡

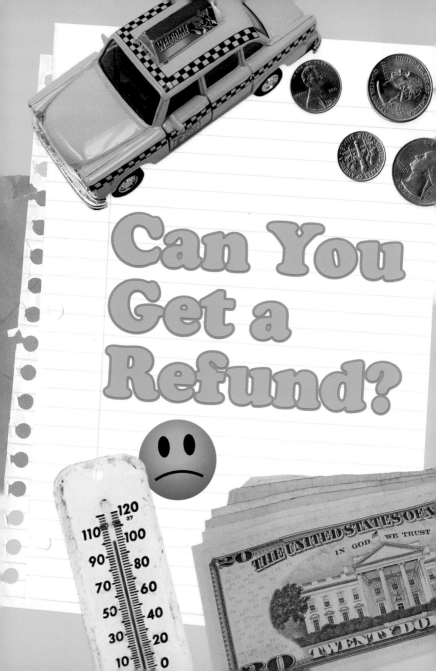

Can You Get a Refund?

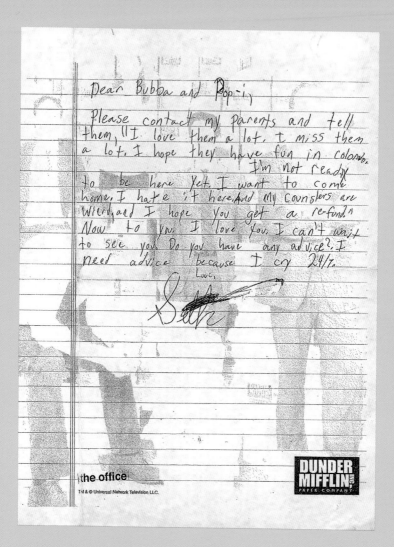

Dear Bubba and Pop-i,

Please contact my parents and tell them, "I love them a lot, I miss them a lot, I hope they have fun in Colorado. I'm not ready to be here yet. I want to come home, I hate it here. And my counslers are wierd, and I hope you get a re-fund." Now to you, I love you. I can't wait to see you. Do you have any advice? I need advice because I cry 24/7.

Love,
Seth

In this envelope, there is a paper that says "Please Read". Don't be alarmed by what it says. I won't take action until I get a reply.

Love,
Noah

Front

Please
Read

Dear Mom and Dad,

This camp is really bad. I can't stay here for $3\frac{1}{2}$ weeks. Please come pick me up. If you do not, I will leave camp by:

Running away

Getting Sick

Contacting the office for help

Please come! I can't stay here!

Love,
Noah

Jacob

☆ ☆

Dear daddy and mommy, Camp has gone from bad to ~~worse~~ worse these are the things that happen in the last 2 day I spranded my pinkie (its not pretend the infermary said I did) I hate all my English****** ~~by~~ conselors they lost all my sox and boxers!!!! I'm so mad. but I'm not done yet I counted and I have 13 mosceto bites most on my neck and I just **plain misrable** its the 3rd

Jacob

day and I definately
do not think I can
survive the summer
please do something.

Love

Jacob

Dear Mom,

I don't want to stay two weeks. Here are the Reasons

1: I almost ~~drowned~~ In the Lake

2: Kayli did a Summer salt on my head

Singed
Your banged
up kid,
Erin

I want to come home so much.

I want to come home
I want to come home
I want to come home
I want to come home
I want to come home
I want to come home

Let me come home
Let me come home
Let me come home

Well g2G

signing out from a
friendless state

Dana

Call the
Officed
tell them
your want to
talk to me

Dear, Mommy,   July 5, 2010

I   I realy miss you
I want you to come get
I am not haveing fun so
far!!   I was crying for you
:(
I have never been this home
sick.   Please come get me
Now!   I'll write you a
letter.   tell Dusty I♥U.

Tell Sean that I♥U Tell daddy
that I ♥U I really missssss
youuuu! ♥U

            Love,
            Malena

Dear Mommy, I miss you
I really, really, really

//// /// //// don't

want you to leave
your cell phone on all
times, so I can call you
but if you need more
batterie charge your
cell phone

Hi   Im stuck in
Hell and they wont
let me call for you to
pick me up so when
you get this pick me
up.

Hi I'm having
the whorst time
of my life. They won't let
me call for you or
my parents pick me up
This pick me up when you get

Week 3

geting a little better
time. can't say ~~xxxxx~~ HOW
many Friends but a few.

Week 4

Having a little better
time still not hevan
but its OK/fun/terribale/
great all mixed together

Wednesday

Dear Papa,

I am having a great time, but I can't wait to go home. The bathrooms are gross, the showers are horrible, & the beds are VERY uncomfortabe!

McKay

Dear Parents

Instead of going to camp for 3$\frac{1}{2}$ weeks can you please pick me up 3 days after you visit? that's 3 weeks (almost). Please, please can you. I hate Many teachers and I only like my counslers. I think 3 people are complete knew-it alls. Please please please, please, carefully consider this. I will beg and pleat for what happens.

Hello, half of me hates this place, and $\frac{1}{4}$ of me is homesick, and $\frac{1}{4}$ of me is having fun, but only about 20% of that $\frac{1}{4}$ is having fun. The rest of me hates everything.

It is 100° and we are burning hot. Pleeassszzz!!!!!!!

Dear Mom
        I wanna come
home. Please let
me come home. I can't
sleep. I really want
to. Please please
please. I want to come
home. And if you do not
take me home send me
ponys.

            Daniel

    I need stamps
        6/29

Dear Mom and Dad,
I'm doing fine. Its pretty fun because
you get a lot of free time to shoot around.
The food is aweful, I live on bread. You
forgot to get me a bob, but I bought one.

Mom and Dad this is about a day later.
And I'm very sick. I couldn't get to sleep at
all and I keep throwing up. The cabins are
aweful and I hate it. I really want to
go home. They lied when they said you
should stay two weeks because each week you
start the same stuff. If hell is a place on
earth this is it. Charlie wants to come home
to but dosn't have a letter. I know you
can't pick us up but I wish you could.
Theres no way I can stay any longer.
please call right when you get this.
       Love, Mickey

75

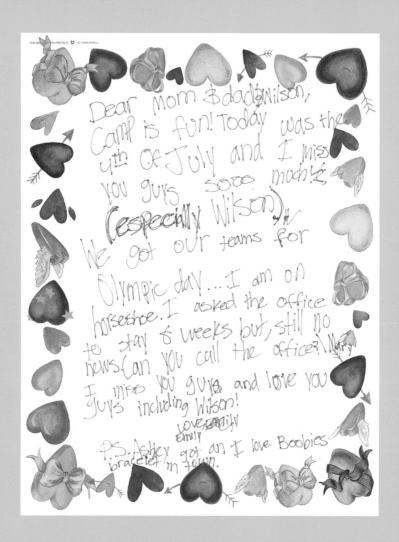

Dear Mom & dad & Wilson,
Camp is fun! Today was the
4th of July and I miss
you guys sooo much!
(especially Wilson)
We got our teams for
Olympic day....I am on
horseshoe. I asked the office
to stay 8 weeks but, still no
news. (Can you call the office?)
I miss you guys and love you
guys including Wilson!
Love,Emily
Emily
P.S. Ashley got an I love Boobies
bracelet in town.

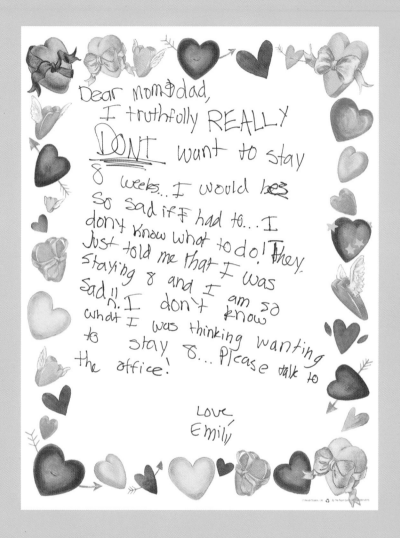

Dear Mom & Dad,
I truthfully REALLY
__DON'T__ want to stay
8 weeks... I would be
so sad if I had to... I
don't know what to do! They
just told me that I was
staying 8 and I am so
sad!! I don't know
what I was thinking wanting
to stay 8... Please talk to
the office!

Love
Emily

Hi Dad!   allie Thank you
for the e-mails, they
always cheer me up,
because they are sooo
funny! I'M STILL EXTREM-
ELY HOMESICK, I Repeat
EXTREMELY HOMESICK!

Dear Dad ant mom,   Day 2

Camp Cody isn't all you say it would be, most
of the good activitys are for teens. only some
of the kids are nice. ~~~~ IN rifalry I hrt all 5
byllets on the target and 2 went in the sang @cccc!
The activitys arn't very fun. The food snt that
good. I dont know how I can have fun the whole time
me and alex are not having a good time. I can't Do
alot Of stuff because on the swim test w/o a life
jacket we hgt go swim 10 you? Size laps
w/o gogles, I can't go knee boardIhg or ☆ water
skiing. see you in 12 days hope they go qutck

        sincerly, Noub

        P.S. I don't like it here

79

Dear, mommee !! :)
mag you please pick me up on friday I miss you sooo much michael went to the docter today and they said his tooth is swolen and they put him on meds if he does not get better

by friday he has to go home and please Let me go to. I hate every thing about this place. Please. Please Please

PICK ME UP

where should I send my Letters to rye or NYC Love, Boho

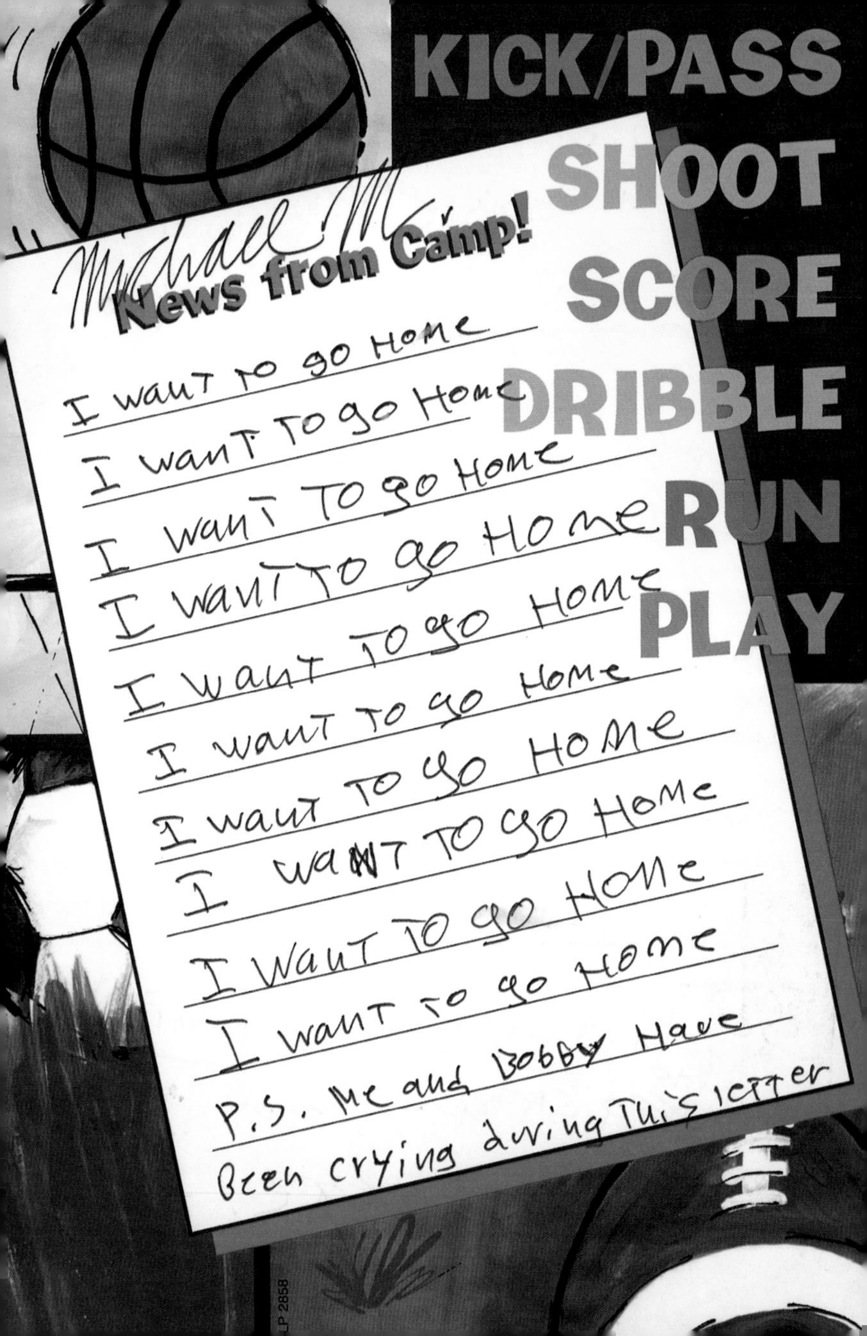

July 20, 1977

Dear Mom, Dad, and Tom,

I'm really homesick. I was even homesicker. I couldn't even eat barely. I really miss you. I'm never going to a camp again. The food's pretty good. I'm taking Arts and Crafts and canoeing as classes. My homesickness is getting better

I'm sending this letter in a different envelope because all my others were sealed from the moisture in the air. I wish you could come and pick me up.

Love,
Mike

84

Dad—

PLEASE GO ME PICK ME UP BEFORE NEXT SAT!

I'm miserable and can't stay here in this dump any longer! I love you + miss you! - XOXO -

Allie

P.S Girls are mean!

Day – Send to mom

Dear mom, ^(and dad) This camp is to long and I want to see you and dad so badly. I cant stop thinking of you and going home. I am only happy doing activities and not thinking of you. Please write back soon!

From alex

P.S. I am angry at dad For sending me here

I MISS YOU TOO MUCH.

I MISS YOU TOO MUCH

PLEASE HELP

DON'T IGNORE THIS LETTER! ME! EMERGENCY LETTE!

I'm really sad!

Day ①, horrible

Dear, Mom & Dad the bus ride
here was terrifying Then I found
out that John was in a different
cabin I said "Yes" but then
I did'nt know anybody and then
John knows everybody ~~too~~ now

I want John in ~~John's~~
cabin my
~~room~~ now

I hate camp

Sincerely, Bub

Dear mom and dad,
I hate it here at camp. i liked your pictures
I had a very bad morning but the
afternoon was not bad. I would still love
for you to pick me up. you must see
happy pictures of me on the website,
he told me 2 smile. My Stomach pains
have increased and I gag every other
20 minutes. I would love it in
your bunk notes for long letters and pictures
I didn't sleep the first night, the day
we arrived, I was crying all night until
dawn, I was supposed to call you today (morning)
but I decided to wait. Please call derek
and remind him to tell miles or the unit
director about how I donot want to go
on the stupid overnighter like I said
before, I would very much love for you
to pick me up days feel like weeks and
I always have bugs on me every night and
during some of the day I pray for you
to pick me up. I usually have serious
Meltdowns maybe 6-8 times a day. I know
My anxiety limit and it is on the verge
of breaking past it. Please do me a favor

and end my pain and call the camp and withdraw me. Please, I beg you. If I come home I promise I'll read and you can take the computer away. PLEASE I only ask of this one thing, I am in pain, would you really want this for your son as a mother? 2 different kids left today. I have more anxiety ITS NOT FAIR! Why me they got lucky because their parents realize they do not like camp and their in pain. you guys just say, you'll get through it. REALIZE I'M IN PAIN!! please help me this once WITHDRAW ME. I BEG YOU.

Dear mom and dad,

I am currently having one of the worst times of my childhood. I cry almost every other minute. Im crying right now and failing asleep is harder than ever. It is worse than last year and i hate it so much. My eyes are so blurry I spell things wrong. I am on the top bunk and there are alot of bugs its very annoying and Im very mad. Im very disapointed that you wouldn't take me home even though I showed so much affection towards home. It is currently 2:40 A.M. and my crying has kept me up. the first night was undescribisley escrutiating. the food is nasty and horrible. I miss you and would like to come. the reason I am talking so calm is because I am trying not to cry but I cannot stop my tent mates are horrible they don't shutyp. you did me no good but woose by sending me even though I demanded to not go. I have thrown up multiple times from Anxiety. I stay by myself and cry and think about how I can enjoy this time but I can't get my mind off home. Days feel like weeks. Sean is crying to at night and I have rubbed off on him. I have apologized to him. My stomach feels like paris 24/7 please pick me up, I can not handle this, I swear on grandma. Please.

Dear. MOMMY and
Daddy. I miss you
alot but having
a lot of fun. It is
rainy but my coensers
are awesome but
my cabin is not so
good I only have
Scooty. Eric and Ari
everybody else I
dont like. Love.
Look on the back. Lvers.

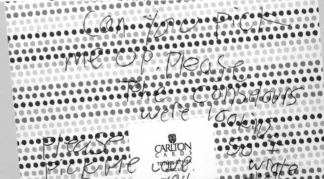

Can you Pick
me Up. Please.
The Conselors
were looking
...
Please
pick me
Up.   you

CARLTON
CARDS

so I
write
that

Aug. 10, 2003
Dear Mommy,

I really want to come home. I miss you a ton. I'm writing this later in the night. Would it be possible for me to come home? Will you get your money back? I've been crying alot but not in Public. I miss you so much. XOXOXO
Love Hilary

Hi...   July 15

    I know you're proud of me
(which you shouldn't be), & I
know you want me to accomp-
lish this; but i don't want to, I
can't, & i won't! Please ... I'll pay
you back, I'll go to piano, & I'll
be good for the rest of my life!!
I promise! Please let me come
home, when you visit! Don't get
me wrong, I'm having fun, but
that's because I know I'm coming
home in one week!

                    ♡ M

Dear mom,

My cold is worse! I hate it here. Who do you care about me or the dumb money, you must care about the money. If you love me you will pick me up, if not I will take a taxi home or ride my bike. I know now that you must not miss me or love me. If you did you would pick me up from this gross!! camp + take me home. My foot is starting to hurt again! I love you.

Sharon

Dear, momeeee!!

can you please pick me up from camp
the guy told me that I can
go home only if you can can
you please call today me and

michael are misrible, and we miss
home please please please come pick
me up before saturday

half the people dont speak english
and I have know freinds and dont
know what a towel is and I
miss you and dad and Josi and Gramps
and NYC Please pick me up
   I Love you sooo much
      I cryed 1000 times
         S. O. S   Love, Bobby

97

Dear mom,

I miss   You so Much call
You come and yet Me Please,
I cant Stand it any more
and   Just ignore what
dad says cause I dont
give a   crap   about it
Just get me out of here.

Dear Mom and Dad,
   Please, you have to get me out of here. You two are the only ones that can do it. It's not that I'm just homesick, it's a word farther then that. I have to get out of here. I promise you, if you don't get me out of here, I'll run away. Please! I'm not kidding. Mom! Dad! I love you. Get me out of here.

Love,
Tim

P.S.: Please talk to my counslers, I just don't belong here.

This Is an Emergency, I Need...

DEAR MOM

THIS IS AN EMERGENCY I NEED A NEW PEN. MY OTHER PEN BROKE AND A NEW LOCK (WITH COMBONATION) AND MORE STAMPS.

SIGN
YOUR LOVEBLE
SON ~~????~~ THE GREAT

Camp news

Dear Mom & Dad,

Hi! Camp is great! Before Jess comes up I need a few things! A big pack of double AA battaries, (they say "AA"), A few more green letters to send letters to you in case I run out. Also I bought a water bottle on thursday at the canteen so I don't need one anymore!!! The letters take 2-4 days to get to you and you can respond quick, but not me, and I have limited writing utensils. So I'm going to write once or twice a week. I love it at camp! Today's Friday Night at shabbot, the food was awesome! I love you, Write back!!!

Love, Danny!

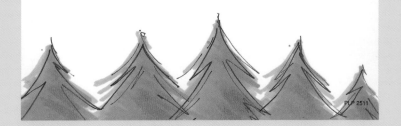

PLP 2511

Dear Dad,
Hi! Once you get this letter could you please send me my yo-yo, it's in my closet.

Thanx,
Nathan

P.S.

Send it ASAP!!!

Florida ♡

♡

Dear mommy, I do miss you and
I still think the new food is iky & Please
send me the new Harry potter book thanks
I still miss you more than
any one I love you
Please to the write
back love always
Shell

Most dolphins grow to approximately six feet in length. Dolphins can be found in
practically all the seas and oceans of the world.

La mayoría de los delfines crecen hasta alcanzar 6 pies de largo aproximadamente.
Los delfines habitan prácticamente casi todos los océanos y mares del mundo.

© DESIGNED and PRINTED by
The Postcard Factory®, 2801 John Street, Markham, Ontario L3R 2Y8 (905) 477-9901   Printed in Canada   Photo: S. Westmorland
Ref: FL-85

P.S. Please
send more stamps
XO thanks.

Dear Mom + Dad,
I nead shoe laces; Friday
is the worst day in wheather
It is foggy but not cold
Otherwise it is warm and
sunny
Love
CAPT

Dear Mom and Dad,
its time for you
to know that
we need a fourth
dog. $ Can we
please please please
please please please
with a cherry
on top get a
black lab?

Dear Mommy + addy,
    Howiis it goin'? Can you
send me some more stamps?
Can you also send bugspray
that repels spiders, long legs, bees,
wasps, hornets, and Jackets! I miss you
guys so much!
        Please visit me soon?
            Love
            Owen

Dear Mom + Dad,
I am getting so hungry
at cabin time and so we are
not allowed to have snaks
an Chukles confiscated my food
inclunding my Phineas+Ferb gummies.
It is so lame at cabin time.
Come visit soon!   Love
XXXXXXXXXXXX   Owen
OOOOOOOOOO

DEAR MA: SUN. 11 (NITE)
I HALF TO WRITE YOU MAINLY
BECOUSE OF A SLIGHT PROBLEM,
I KEEP LOSING THINGS, FIRST
MY TOOTHPASTE THAN MY
TOOTHBRUSH, "I AM GOING
CRAZY" AFTER ALL THAT
BRACE WORK MY TEETH
ARE GOING TO **ROT** AWAY,
SO PLEASE, PLEASE, PLEASE,
PLLLEASE SEND ME THOSE
ECCENTIAL INSTRUMENTS AS
SOON AS POSSIBLE.

Can nana send me more night
Pads for sleeping like what
mommy gave me and tampons.
Grandpa and nana
Love and miss ♡
UL!

© 2009 USPS ♻ recycled

109

Arielle

Dear Dad,

I got your lovely package today! But now the consulers open them first, and the entire thing smelled like the gum. They confiscated it. :(Thanks for the thought tho! Next time, odorless please ☺

XOXO,

Arielle

Dear Mom And dAd The PeRSon fRom The PicLuRe WAS My fRiend CoRy fRom ELoRidA You didn7 PACK Me ANY BOXERS CAn you Send uP Like A Bizzilion fRom my chAiR ToDAy i did 3 hundRed ~~SiTuPS~~ SiTuPS My goAl is To hAve A Six PACK AT The end of SummeR.

Love

TyLeR

A Note From...

Dear mom,
sorry havent
been writing, havent
gotten to it.
   I forgot a few
thing on My List.
cup noodles Mac cheese
raman noodles, If I
already had those I'm
sorry aๆ bring bum
and starbursts. one
more thing bring
the most important
thing yourseff
!!!   Love
   Jacob

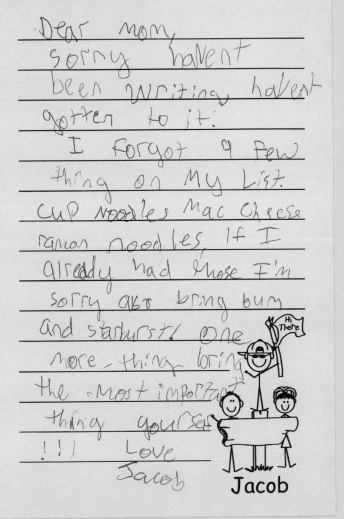

Jacob

Dear mom we do the [postmark]
same thing where
we change gender
so can you bring
a wig and a dress
that fit me on
visiting day.
from charlie

33326+3503

ADDRESS

Dear mommy, Daddy & CO
I love you (miss you
a lot, lot, lot, lot, lot
lot, lot, lot, lot, lot, lot
lot, lot and nommy

P.S. Fight back
you pleaseplease

7/16/05

ADDRESS

can you pleasesent
me a ClipFan you know
one thats alittle big and
you clipon

you can analyze but I would like you to try to bring all of it.

Food List

split the food with Roberta - from Lauren

Bagles and Bialies and crossiants
Cheese, cream cheese, margarine
Chicken scaparilla (La Parma)
Cheese Bread, Pasta (La Parma)
Cottage Fries, Fried onions, Hash browns (Bryant + Cooper)
(Dursos) cheese sticks
Pickles, Pepperoni, salami, coleslaw, chopliver
(Polutry Mart) Eli's bread, Noodle Pudding
Smartfood Popcorn, Pretzels, sour creme and onion potatoe chips, chocolate covered pretzels
Trail Mix
Diet Coke
Entemans chocolate crunch cake or chocolate chip pound cake, brownie cookies
Sald (MARC) Dole - Cesar or Oriental (Any fruit too grapes ect.)
Matzah Brie

Dear Dad & Mom,
Right now I am ~~writing~~
writing you this from the Infirmary.
I am staying here for the
night because I have strep
throat. It stinks. I am very ~~bored~~
bored. Thankyou so much for the
stamps by the way. I just
got them and it made me
feel 100x better knowing
that you love me. By the way
I don't want to be picky
but I might need some
more stamps. I am going on a
trip in 4 days. Can you believe
it. I miss you sooooo much.
I Love you soooooooooo much.
I wish you were here.

...YOU'RE LOOKING BETTER
THAN EVER, DEARIE!

TUESDAY.

HI EVERYBODY

WHATS NEW? I HAVN'T GOT MUCH TO SAY
BUT GEUSS WHAT? SOMEBODY STOLE MY
PEN A DOLLER AND A STAND FROM ME
SO COULD YOU PLEASE SEND ME
SOME STAMPS BECOUSE I HAVE NO MORE
LEFT (I BORROWED A STAMP AND A PEN) WELL
I HAVN'T GOT ANYTHING ELSE TO SAY
SO BYE NOW

DAVID

WRITE SOON

I ♡

CAMP

♡ Bianca

P.S. remember to send cookies

Dear Family,   6/23/09
Camp is superb. I have not actually
dived yet, but, I learned in a class-
room. I have taken 3 quizzes and
I got 100% on all of them. Also,
I haven't gotten hurt yet. Please
send cookies. Gavin, my counselor,
is really nice. Cris, my other
counselor, is not as nice and is
strict.
                        Love, Dylan

Dear mom and dad,
Camp rocks. I got around on wake board. We're going to the dunes tomorrow. colordaze are soon. I'm sad it's almost over. Michael came back. He had ammonia for two weeks.
Love,
Matt

Dear mom & dad,
Hi, I have bball leagues today. I'm pumped. I got to go. Sorry this was a crappy letter.
♡ Matt

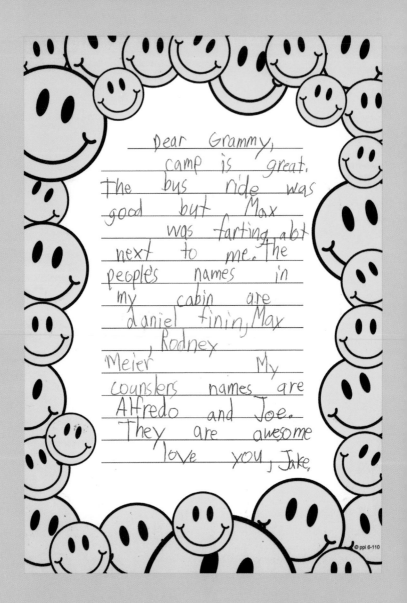

Dear Grammy,
camp is great. The bus ride was good but Max was farting a lot next to me. The people's names in my cabin are daniel finin, Max, Rodney Meier My counslers names are Alfredo and Joe. They are awesome love you, Jake.

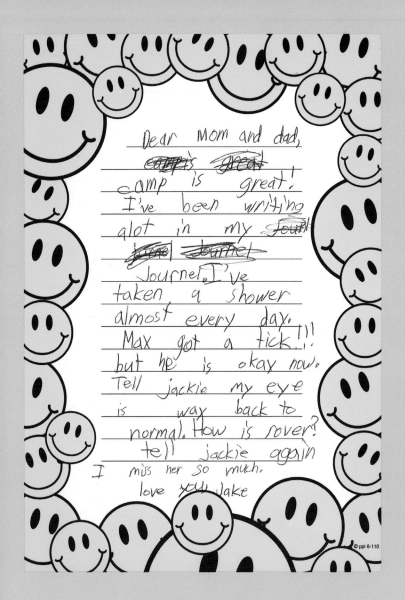

Dear Mom and dad,
~~camp is~~ ~~green~~
camp is great!
I've been writing
alot in my ~~fourth~~
~~funny~~ ~~journel~~
Journel. I've
taken a shower
almost every day.
Max got a tick!!!
but he is okay now.
Tell jackie my eye
is way back to
normal. How is rover?
tell jackie again
I miss her so much.
love ~~you~~ Jake

© ppi 6-110

June 20, 76

Dear Mom and Dad,

The plane ride was nice.

The weather is nice.

The Camp is great.

It is beautiful I Love it
pleas send me some mad's.

You know what, I was
getting settled and taking out
stuff and my koetg propped
out on the floor!
the Food is good
we had peanut Butter
+ Jelly I ate it
I met a girl her
name is Ronna she
is really nice!,

Dear mom. I have lots of freindst
We've got namms for everyor we
call Mathew. Smile we gall
Job soggy Woodel we
cell Brad

Braedely the friendy
Gohst we cpll mop dopery
gillies we gall victore Mose

and ferry Horse

and Micth and dave
don't have a name

A Note From...

6/26/04

Dear Mommy
I am having a BLAST
but girls are being mean
and yelling at me
but otherwise its
fineo Really nothing
else to say.

Love

Sammi

Samantha

Dear Mom & Dad
I am having so much
fun. A kid got sent home.
I am also taking guitar.
I learned 3 songs in
A period. There are no cicadas
up here. How are they
at home?

Dear Mom + Dad
Camp's great! I am doing awesome
in waterskiing. I lost a tooth
at the dunes yesterday Love you
                Bye
                Andy

Dear Mom & Dad
So far camp is ~~good~~ great I love all
the kids in my cabin. I made
a friend from St. Louis his name is
Sam. He says SL is awesome. They
made the Dinning hall bigger.
Some nights they will have
a potato bar. I love you.

Love,
Andrew

Dear Mom, Dad, Joey, and Nate
Last night was cornnight
when A girls camp And
was there. Tonight
is karcokee night and
our cabin is doing the song
Fish Heads. It's chorous
is: Fish Heads, Fish Heads,
roly poly fish Heds. Fish he
ads, fish heads, Eat them up,
yum! Were going to win
best act.

David

Dear Mom, Dad, Joe, Nute, and Helga,
What's up at home? There is a lot going on here! I just got back from my 3 night trip to Trout Lake It was incredible!!!!!!!!! One kid was minorly struk by lightning during a scary, windy, rainy storm, but otherwise it was really fun swimming in the rapids, and paddling them. Also, last night was carni-night and a girl's camp came over. I got my fortune told and I was to be a rich wealthy man! Camp is great and I love you guys.

Love,
David

Dear Sandra,
I LOVE camp but I also miss home.
I keep trying to water ski, but I fall the second the boat moves. Well, I'll try again today. I just made a rocket called the Gemini DC. Can you please send me a picture of you?

David

127

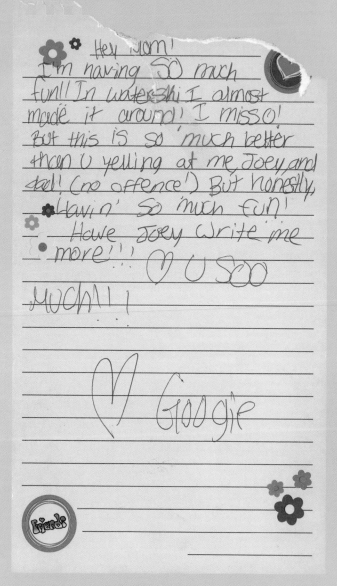

Hey Mom!

I'm having SO much fun!! In water-ski I almost made it around! I miss O! But this is so much better than U yelling at me, Joey, and dad! (no offence!) But honestly, Havin' so much fun!

Have Joey write me more!!! ♡ U SOO MUCH!!!

♡ Googie

Love,
Jake

enough

Dear Mom
I will already be home but thank you for sending me hear, I am having a great time! I am very thankful for all of this. I am sorry if I did not write alot of letters. THANK YOU, SO MUCH!

Love,
Charlie

Hi from...CAMP!

Dear family,
I ♡ Camp! It's the best!
The second I got on the bus I
knew this was the place to be!

I ♡ and miss you.
☺ Emily

Dear Mom,
I am coming
home today!
GARY

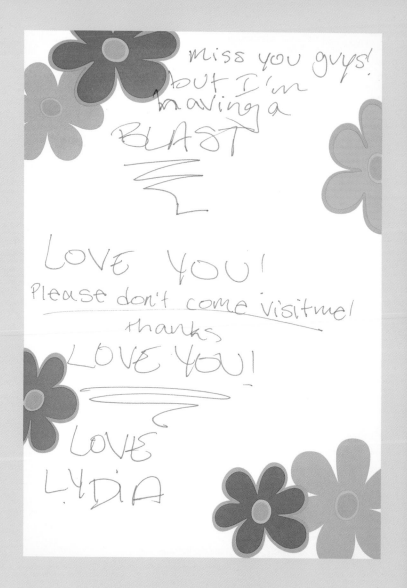

miss you guys!
but I'm
having a
BLAST

LOVE YOU!
Please don't come visit me!
thanks
LOVE YOU!

LOVE
LYDIA

Sibs, Pets & Miscellaneous Missives

Dear emily,
i miss
you very much
I hope you
are taking
showers!
LOVe,
Lexi

Emily

134

Dear Katie,
   Camp is great! Tell Sarah, abby, hannah,
and   nathalie that I   am   totally interested
but   ~~the~~ tell me ~~in~~ where they live
and   there phone numbers. Also tell me which
one   is the hottest in your opinion.
~~Not lesbin~~ It   won't count ~~that~~ as a lesbo
if   you tell   me. My favorite food
here   is ~~that~~ still coffee cake.
Also I   think I   am getting
a   ~~box~~ really awesome 6 pack and
my   ~~need~~ muscles got bigger.
I   have been going   to sailing a lot!

I   like to go sailing but not
~~~~ to sail boats.

           I   ♡   U (and your friends),

           Love

           J- dawg
             Jake
P.S. Can you send me   your iPod!

A Note From... Tony

Dear Mom and dad

Camp is cool ~~Big~~ Sammi
has a boyfriend
his name is Zach
dont tell her
that if you
do...

see you
later!

Hi There

Andrew

A Note From...

Dear Mommy
I want to Know
if I can
SHAVE

Love   Its a razor
                    without a blade
    Sammi   Its called
                    veet

Pine Forest Camp

Samantha

7/28/11

Dear Ben,

I hate camp. I hate the overcrowded bunk, the people aren't super nice except some of them. I have really painful rope burn on 3 fingers and I have to constantly put ice on them. Thanks for sending me a note. I miss you so much. I can't believe i still have 10 days left. I'm so happy I didn't sign up for the 4 week session. I'm trying to not celebrate my birthday here. I like to be with my family on birthday, not a bunch of obnoxious 11 year olds that I barely know. So I'm illegally

Moving my birthday to August 8th. I'm gonna skype dad. When you and mom come up for me, will you bring ~~the other~~ the iTouch, and my phone+ charger? So my icepack just spilled all over my bed and my fingers really hurt. Camp smells bad. Gotta go to lunch now, bye. I miss you

Love,
Matty.

Dear Jake
because you
took Dreamer
you made
my life
misrabull
cincerly Katie

Dear Family,

I want to talk to Toto! "Hi Toto. How is it going? Good. I am glad to hear that. I know Toto. I miss you too. Toto can you please put Spunky on the letter, thanks. Hi Spunky. I know. You miss me too. But I am running out of paper. So let me talk to mom or dad or the whole family. O.k. the whole family." I miss you family, and I hope to see you soon. When you come to pick me up bring, Toto, pickles, peppers, or Salt n' Vinegear chips. Any of them will satisfy me. Thanks. I love you.

Love,

Tamara

Dear Thomas and Joe
Thank you so much
for the pink
pillow pet pig!
If I didn't have
it- I swear- I
wouldn't be able
to sleep as well
as now. It is
so soft and
amazing so thanks.
I am so lucky to
have you as brothers.
I miss you
SOOOOO
—————
much!
    -Kate

Dear Mom+Dad,

Max has been on a trip for 2 day but I will make sure I get the magizine to him. Max has been a great brother in as many ways as posible. He diserves alot of credit.

Love,
Chawlie

143

happy birthday

Dear Dad,
HAPPY BIRTHDAY! I love you so much,
and you're the best dad EVER! I hope
you have an awesome birthday, and
I'm sorry I can't celebrate with
you while I'm at camp! LOVE YOU!
　　　　-Anna :‍:
P.S. now that you're legally considered
"a middle aged man" make sure you go
through your "mid-life crises" while
I'm still at camp! ♡

Kate

Dear Violet,

How are you doing so far? I know swimming in a fish bowl is boring-just hang in there. Also- write to me if Dad is feeding you to much Pellets. Don't let him kill you. I will be back soon!

-Kate

Dear Lexi, (Mom & dad can read it)
I miss you so much! You are an
awesome sister. I hope that you
come next year so that I
could be with you all summer!
If you don't come I will probably stay home with you. I miss
you and love you!
                    Love,
                    Emily

Dear Mom & dad (parents (wonderful))
I miss you guys so much. Today
we had ~~late~~ lazy Sunday
I had one chocolate pancake and
one blueberry pancake (there were
no more strawberry) But they
were really good.

                    Love,
                    Emily.

P.S. Send me a picture of
Mom, Dad and LEXI. I miss
Lexiz so much. (didn't know
that I would miss her this
much. Bring her on visiting
weekend.

I am
having the best
time of my life!
I don't know why
I'm going now I
should of went
three years ago.

LOVE,
Lexi

English

FRIDAY, 19/6/2011

Dear family,

I miss you a lot.

Mum you help me always.

Dad you make me always.
Vera you bring me always.
Granfather Bruno and Grandmother Gianna
thank you for all the presents.
Thank you Granfather Valfrido for all
the ghifts gifts that you made me.
Belba cat dear I miss your purreng.
I am like one pencil wi out point and
you are a sharpner.
I am like one shower wi out water and you are
plumber.

I am like one house wi out foundation and you are
builder.
I am like one pen wi out ink you are
cartridge.

FROM BRUNO

Italiano

Venerdì, 19/6/2011

Cara famiglia,
Mi mancate molto.
Mamma tu mi aiuti sempre.
Papà tu mi fai sempre felice.
Vera tu mi sostieni sempre
Nonno Bruno è Nonna Gianna
grazie per tutti i regali.
Grazie nonno Valfrido per tutti
i doni che tu mi fai.
Belba cara gatta e me mancano le tue fusa.
Io sono come una matita senza punta e voi siete
il temperino
Io sono come una doccia senza acqua e voi siete
l'idraulico.
Io sono come una casa senza fondamenta e voi siete
il costruttore.
Io sono come penna senza inchiostro e voi siete
la ricarica

DA BRUNO

Shelby

Dear everyone,

right me
Please Please

| | | | | |
| | | | | |

Love ya

Mom

XXX OOO
XXX OOO

149

P.S

I am only smiling
in the pictures so you
think I am having tons
of fun... But i'm not.

P.S. I miss you
sorry ~~so~~ about the
letter but someone did threaten
to kill me but she was all
talk. Love you,
Shelsea.

P.S. I have a infected foot and a really bad feaver! ☺

P.S. We should got a pingpong table for home. Please!!!!!!!!

P.S. please send me a letter I'm the only one in my cabin that has not gotten a letter

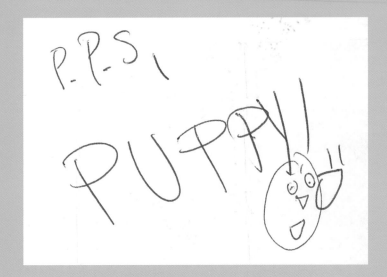

P.P.S.

PUPPY!!

P.S. I really need a
Flashlight. they don't work
that well (almost out). (dim).

(P.S. don't send candy! it's a law here. And,
the flashlight u sent has a burnt bulb.
We tried everything.)

P.S

I had a dream last night that I ran off the bus to see you at the end of camp and you surprised me+max with a doggie. will that happen?. PLEASE!!?. I know its a alot of work and dad isnt home alot, but I promise that I will take care of it. If not now, then when dad finishes traveling? I ♡ U!

xoxo,
Maya

P.S. send me some clothes, glasses, or Hats to make me look like a gambler for casino night.

P.S. - Bling Bling 4 Jesus!

P.S. The water is freezing cold in the lake
P.P.S. Have fun in San Fran while I get bitten by mosquitos.

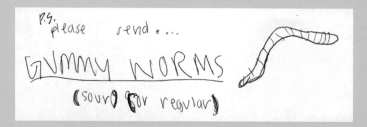

P.S.
please send...

GUMMY WORMS
(sour) (or regular)

P.S. I'm sending
you raindrops

Gotta Go,
Love,
Eryn.
P.S. Write Back please
P.P.S. Send me a package please
P.P.P.S Make a call back please
P.P.P.P.S Camp is great

P.s. tell Jess to bring her squishie Pillow the great/pink one! It helps! bye!!!

P.S. I am not Dead!!

P.S was that a good letter?

P.P.S.
Thank You

To Billy Kingsland and David Kuhn at Kuhn Projects—thank you for helping this second volume come to life and for laughing with me at the hilarious new camp letters. Thanks to Lucy Stille at Paradigm for optioning the television rights for *P.S. I Hate It Here: Kids' Letters from Camp* to Original Productions and ABC to adapt for Disney Television.

A huge thank-you to my terrific editorial, design, marketing, sales, publicity, and production team at Abrams Image: Rebecca Kaplan, Jennifer Levesque, Danielle Young, Kerry Liebling, Amy Lombardi, Claire Bamundo, and Julie Thomson. I couldn t ask to be working with better, more creative people.

To my extraordinary friends—you know who you are—thank you for your constant support, wit, and wisdom. And to the camps nationwide that helped me locate letters, I can't thank you all enough. (Camp Medolark and Scott Weinstein—I would be particularly lost without you.) Thank you to Dayna Hardin and the American Camp Association for inviting me to do a camp letters reading at the national meeting in San Diego, and for introducing me to so many camp directors nationwide. Also, to my fabulous family and relatives, thank you all for your continued enthusiasm and genuine excitement.

A big thank you to everyone who sent me their wonderfulfamily camp letters. I received thousands from across the country—it's always so hard to choose. Also a special note to all the campers out there: Thank you for going to camp and writing home often.

Finally, to Mark, Blake, and Bianca—you are still my all-time favorite people to camp with. Thank you for loving this project, again. I love you.

P.S. Mom, this one's for you.

Editor: Rebecca Kaplan
Designer: Danielle Young
Production Manager: Julie Thomson

Published in 2012 by Abrams Image
An imprint of ABRAMS

Cataloging-in-Publication Data has been applied for and may
be obtained from the Library of Congress.

ISBN: 978-1-4197-0279-2

Printed and bound in Mexico
10 9 8 7 6 5 4 3 2 1

Abrams Image books are available at special discounts
when purchased in quantity for premiums and promotions
as well as fundraising or educational use. Special editions
can also be created to specification. For details, contact
specialsales@abramsbooks.com or the address below.

THE ART OF BOOKS SINCE 1949
115 West 18th Street
New York, NY 10011
www.abramsbooks.com